# DEMETER'S SEARCH FOR PERSEPHONE

## Mythology 4th Grade
## Children's Greek & Roman Books

**BABY PROFESSOR**
EDUCATION KIDS

Speedy Publishing LLC

40 E. Main St. #1156

Newark, DE 19711

www.speedypublishing.com

Copyright 2017

In this book, we're going to talk about the story of Demeter's search for Persephone. So, let's get right to it!

The story of Demeter and her daughter Persephone was at the core of the religious beliefs of the ancient Greeks. The story was the heart of the Eleusinian Mysteries. These mysteries were a series of sacred ceremonial rituals that were held every year. Their purpose was to give the people who participated a chance for rebirth into a better life after death.

# WHO WAS DEMETER?

The word "meter" in the Greek language means "mother." Demeter was the goddess of the harvest and agriculture. She was very important and powerful because without a fruitful harvest there would be no food for the Greeks to eat and no work to keep the farmers employed.

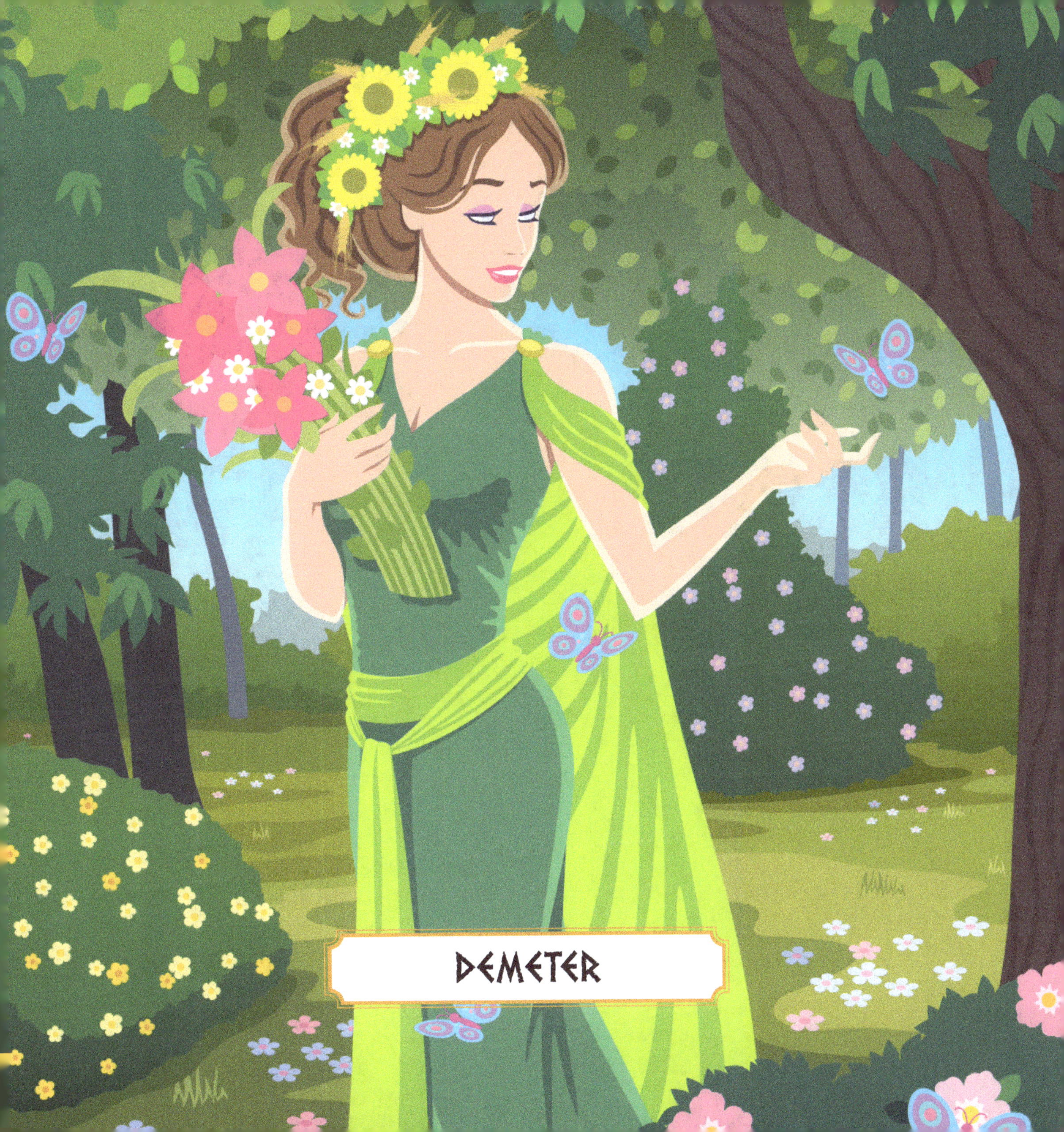

DEMETER

Demeter was the sister of both Zeus and Hera. Zeus was the god of all the Greek gods and Hera, was his wife and also his sister. Along with them, Demeter was one of the first generation of goddesses.

She had been swallowed by Kronos, who was the Titan father of them all. Her brother Zeus, who had not been swallowed, had freed her. Unlike the other goddesses on Mount Olympus, Demeter was not a maiden and she wasn't married either.

STATUE OF DEMETER

Demeter was in love with Iasion. He was the prince of the island of Krete and he wasn't a god. He was a mortal man.

When Zeus found out that Iasion had been with his sister, he got very angry and decided to kill him with a thunderbolt.

PERSEPHONE

He decided to take his other sister Demeter for himself as well. Zeus was never loyal to his wife and sister, Hera. Hera was very jealous and she often sought revenge against Zeus. This is a recurring theme in Greek mythology. The result of the coupling of Zeus and Demeter was their daughter, Persephone, the goddess of spring.

# HADES, THE GOD OF THE UNDERWORLD

Hades was the god of the Underworld. He was also the brother of Zeus, Hera, and Demeter as well as Persephone's uncle. He watched Persephone from a distance as she grew up and became very beautiful.

HADES

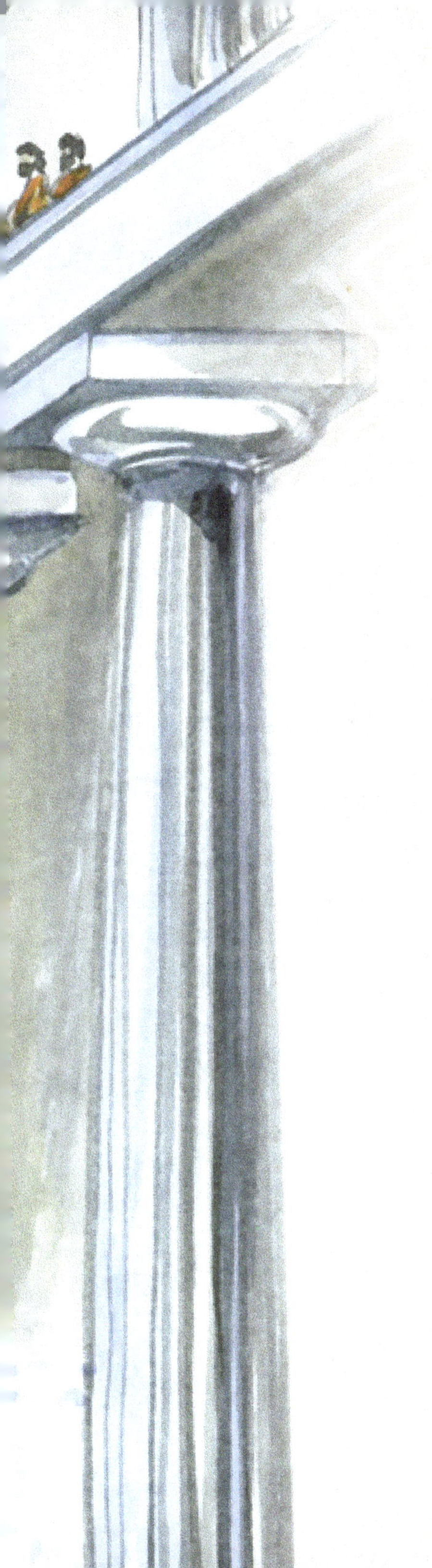

He went to ask Zeus if he would give her in marriage, because he wanted her to be his wife and live in the Underworld with him. Zeus didn't tell Demeter that he was going to give his permission. In fact, he kept it a secret from her.

# HADES KIDNAPS PERSEPHONE

One day, Persephone was out on a meadow hillside. She was happily plucking wildflowers with her friends. Then, without any warning, the ground opened up underneath her feet and her uncle Hades, the King of the Afterlife, grabbed her and took her down to the Underworld in his horse-driven chariot.

HADES KIDNAPS PERSEPHONE

PERSEPHONE WAS KIDNAPPED

Persephone was terrified as she was taken down under the surface of the Earth into the darkness. She called out to her father Zeus, but he refused to answer her since he had given his permission to Hades.

He was sheltered in one of the temples where the mortals were bringing offerings to him. The sun god, Helios, saw what had happened and so did Hekate, the goddess of the moon.

HEKATE

DEMETER MOURNING FOR PERSEPHONE

# DEMETER GOES IN SEARCH OF HER DAUGHTER

At the last second before Persephone went under the ground, Demeter heard her cry. Demeter flung off her veil and her heavy cloak and flew over the lands and the seas in search of the daughter she loved.

For nine days and nine nights, she traveled over the Earth with two torches, one in each hand. She was overcome with grief at the loss of Persephone. She asked everyone she met, mortal or god, what had occurred.

Those she met didn't know what had happened or if they did they were too afraid that Hades would come after them so they didn't tell.

Demeter was so upset that she proclaimed she would destroy the entire Earth and all mortals along with it if she didn't find her daughter. Along the way to show she meant what she said, she began to level the crops and kill the livestock.

HEKATE

# DEMETER MEETS HEKATE

On the tenth day, in the morning, Demeter encountered the goddess Hekate. Hekate told Demeter that she had heard her daughter's screams as she was being kidnapped, but she didn't know who had kidnapped her.

The two goddesses joined forces and went to see Helios, the mighty sun god, who was able to see everything happening on Earth as he was seated on his chariot. Helios told the goddesses what he had seen.

HELIOS

He tried to convince Demeter that the god of the dead wasn't a bad match for her daughter since he was the brother of Zeus and Demeter's brother as well. After all, everyone would meet with the god of the Underworld at one point, so he was very powerful.

After they talked, Helios traveled across the sky in his chariot. By this time, Demeter had realized that Zeus had given his permission to Hades and she was furious with him. She turned her back on the gods and changed herself into a mortal.

# KING CELEUS AND QUEEN METANEIRA

Demeter had disguised herself as an old woman. She traveled to Eleusis, a city near the important city of Athens. She found some shade under a tree to rest. The four daughters of King Celeus and Queen Metaneira came to the nearby well to get some water. When they saw Demeter there, they asked her who she was and invited her to come into the town.

Demeter asked them if they knew anyone who needed a nurse or a housekeeper. One of the daughters told her that their mother had just given birth to a son, named Demophoon. Demeter told her that she would be happy to be a nurse for Demophoon. Metaneira's daughters hurried home to tell her. Metaneira decided that she wanted to hire Demeter who had told the girls her name was Doso instead of giving her real name.

# DEMETER AT THE PALACE

When Demeter got to the palace, Queen Metaneira was sitting next to a pillar as she cuddled her son, Demophoon in her arms.

Metaneira offered her guest a beautiful place to sit as well as food and drink, but Demeter, now known as Doso, wouldn't take any of these things.

AMBROSIA

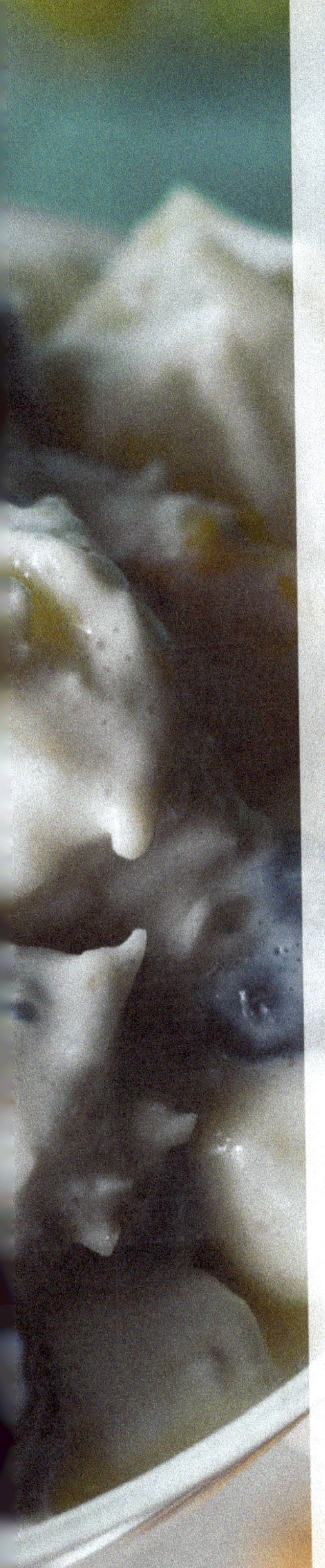

She was still filled with grief at the loss of her own child, Persephone. Finally, a servant woman by the name of Iambe entertained the goddess and got her to smile and laugh a little. Then, Demeter accepted a beverage of mint mixed with barley. Demeter took excellent care of Demophoon. She anointed him with the food of the gods, which was ambrosia. She breathed divine powers into him so he seemed more like a god than an ordinary child. Metaneira was curious about how Demeter was having this effect on her son, so one night she spied on them.

As she was watching and hidden from view, she saw his nurse dangling the baby in the fire. She cried out in anguish because she didn't want her child to be killed. Demeter said to her, "You mortals are so foolish! I was giving immortality to your son, so he would be like a god, but you have stopped me and as a result he will die as all mortals do."

DEMETER AND DEMOPHOON

Then, she emerged from her disguise and showed herself as a goddess with bright light and a beautiful fragrance. She told them that they must build a temple structure in her honor next to the palace. The citizens of Eleusis began building the temple the next day.

# DEMETER MAKES THE WORLD STARVE

In her newly built temple at Eleusis, Demeter continued to rant with rage and grief about the loss of Persephone. She wouldn't allow any crops to grow and mankind was beginning to starve. The gods and goddesses were no longer receiving offerings at the temples.

Zeus realized that a compromise would be needed. He sent many gods to offer gifts to Demeter so that she would return to Mount Olympus, but she refused.

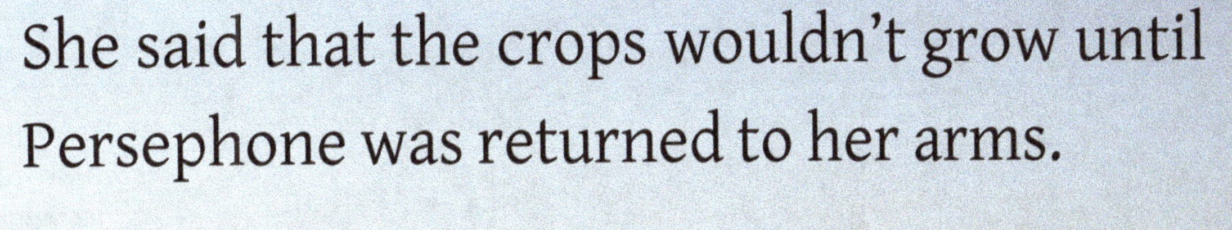

She said that the crops wouldn't grow until
Persephone was returned to her arms.

# THE RETURN OF PERSEPHONE

It was clear that Demeter would not change her mind and something had to be done. Rhea, the goddess mother of Zeus, Demeter, and Hades brokered the compromise. Persephone would come home to her mother for the spring and summer and then go back to her husband in the Underworld for the fall and winter. Every year, when Persephone goes back to the Underworld, the leaves die and the Earth becomes barren and cold to show her mother's grief until she returns.

# THE REUNION OF PERSEPHONE AND DEMETER

# SUMMARY

The goddess of agriculture, Demeter, was very powerful and critical to the citizens of the country of Greece. It was Demeter who had control over their yearly harvest. Demeter was one of Zeus's sisters, but she and Zeus had a daughter together. Their daughter was Persephone, the beautiful maiden goddess of spring.

Without Demeter's knowledge, Zeus said that Persephone's uncle, Hades, king of the Underworld, could have her as his bride. Hades kidnapped Persephone and Demeter was filled with grief at the loss of her daughter. Eventually, they came to a compromise. During the fall and winter, Persephone would rule with Hades in the Underworld and then in spring and summer she would join her mother. This is the story of how the seasons came to be.

# PERSEPHONE IN THE UNDERWORLD

Awesome! Now that you've read about the story of Demeter and Persephone, you may want to read another mythology story in the Baby Professor book, The Marriage of Aphrodite and Hephaestus - Mythology and Folklore | Children's Greek & Roman Books.

Visit

# www.BabyProfessorBooks.com

to download Free Baby Professor eBooks
and view our catalog of new and exciting
Children's Books